Spirit and Flesh, Englishman and Greek

David Roomy

iUniverse, Inc.
Bloomington

Spirit and Flesh, Englishman and Greek

iUniverse books may be ordered through booksellers or by contacting:

iUniverse
1663 Liberty Drive
Bloomington, IN 47403
www.iuniverse.com
1-800-Authors (1-800-288-4677)

Because of the dynamic nature of the Internet, any web addresses or links contained in this book may have changed since publication and may no longer be valid. The views expressed in this work are solely those of the author and do not necessarily reflect the views of the publisher, and the publisher hereby disclaims any responsibility for them.

Any people depicted in stock imagery provided by Thinkstock are models, and such images are being used for illustrative purposes only.

Certain stock imagery © Thinkstock.

ISBN: 978-1-4620-2085-0 (sc)
ISBN: 978-1-4620-2087-4 (hc)
ISBN: 978-1-4620-2086-7 (e)

Printed in the United States of America

iUniverse rev. date: 05/24/2011

In the movie Zorba the Greek, *Alexis Zorba and a bookish Englishman form two parts of a single whole. I hope to spark the reader's interest in finding these two contrasting parts in his or her being. For so many people in our age of darkness, Nikos Kazantzakis's* Zorba the Greek *may be a hopeful icon. I have the audacity to write about Zorba only because I recognize the importance of the bookish part in me. That part is akin to my love for England, so I have represented "Greece" and "England" in this collection of narratives and poems.*

Acknowledgments

The movie *Zorba the Greek* (1964) is based on the novel of the same name by Nikos Kazantzakis. The film, directed by Michael Cacoyannis, features Anthony Quinn as Zorba and the English actor Alan Bates as the intellectual. My copy of the novel was published by Ballantine Books by arrangement with Simon and Schuster, New York (April 1965).

Dedication

The one who by my
pillow lies,
that one I long to see,
the face that sailed this
elfin ship
upon a Grecian sea.

I look and wait my time
when I
my own door open free
and smile upon the face
and lips
of she who waits for me.

The bottle set a note
asail
to distant land or lee,
and hie to other shore,
awash
"a treasure read," wrote
he.

When you return your
way to home,
remember, ever be
what you longed for in
ev'ry trip:
her love, protector be.

CHAPTER ONE
Greece

It takes many people to tell about Greece.

I will tell you about Greece in the words and experiences of four architects who went there with me.

The essence of these words and stories comes from conversations in Greek restaurants and tavernas under summer skies.

The four architects have different points of view; each went seeking something, and each found something different—not just from one another, but from what they were seeking.

That is Greece.

They were in the airport bus that ferries travellers from planes to terminals. In the evening sun, the Athens terminal shone almost like midday. Aristotle, one of the four American architects, boomed, "But I *am* Greek!"

Only a few minutes before, he had told his friends about a dream he had had just before coming to Greece. In the dream he said, "I am Greek," and an old man challenged him with "You don't speak Greek, you are not second-generation Greek-American, and your family are no longer Orthodox." In the dream, Aristotle had stood up and, staring the old man down, insisted, "I *am* Greek!" It was at this point in the retelling on the bus that Aristotle's voice rose.

ϾϪ

But Aristotle had his doubts too. The river of noise outside his hotel window intensified his fears. What if he couldn't sleep? Reading *Zorba the Greek* in bed at 2:30 a.m. was no comfort. Would his earache get worse? Would he be able to find a doctor in the little town where he was going? It was strange, he thought, to come to Greece looking for his spiritual heritage. What was even stranger, he thought as his misgivings really took hold of him, was that he should conceive of such a search as one that could be synchronistic with the search of some of the monastic communities who were looking to early Greek Christianity as an alternative to a spiritually bereft West. The noise of the people below and the cacophony of unmuffled mopeds reminded him of sounds cascading off canyon walls, a deep and desperate noise that invited a desperate plunge. He couldn't let down his anima, his soul, by giving up on his vision.

When he finally slept, he dreamed of a single tear, the love between his wife and him. Light went into it, and it turned into a diamond, indestructible. His deep sleep, although short, seemed like hours, and during this sleep appeared a powerful spiritual figure from Greece itself, a man in gold robes, a monk, carved out of Greek rock, strong, able to hold his spirituality within his powerful torso. He gave something to Aristotle, as Aristotle later told us. It was a miracle: the figure took up residence in Aristotle's body, and the force of all of its power formed in Aristotle's legs and pelvis.

ϾϪ

Homer was one of those solid Americans whose family had been on the North American continent long enough for him to carry himself without apology—a man whose suits were worn but of the finest quality. Homer knew Jean Paul Sartre and Graham Greene and had been to parties with T.S. Eliot. He was studying Greek, and he knew more about Greece than any of the others, although he had no particular connection with the country. In fact, his nose, with its hazardous bend, identified him as a member of an Ayrshire clan.

He told the others that C.G. Jung had told him that what was special about the Greeks among all Westerners was that they had never had a Reformation. The Greeks were still in touch with all their gods, all their instincts. For them, there was no radical break between the mind and the patterns that had governed and guided their lives through the centuries.

One evening Homer met a Zorba-like character. He described the experience to us by reading aloud a letter he was sending home:

> Last night I had an unbelievable experience—one of those things that happen sometimes. Greece was playing Russia in the European soccer finals, and when Greece won, all the Greeks went crazy mad. You can't imagine the noise—everyone honking their horns, the streets filled, cars driving absolutely wild. I met a couple of black Canadians in my hotel and suggested we go to the Plaka. Our hotel was on a very busy city artery that came down from the stadium, and I got a cab just as the crowd broke loose and was piling out. Yes, the driver would take us to the Plaka, about four kilometres away. Horns were blowing, and he was wild, screaming, "Greece is number one!" Then he said, "You won't be able to get back from the Plaka tonight because all the taxis will go on vacation." Then he said, "I will get you back." It was one of those wild, generous things.
>
> I said, "We don't have much money," but it turned out he charged about the regular price. It was true that no one else was working. On the avenue as we were returning from the Plaka, I noticed that everyone was walking—no taxis.
>
> I have experienced Greece when it was wild, ecstatic!

The Athenians like to spend time at Syntagma Square, also called Constitution Square. Foreigners gather there, sitting at the small tables with small glasses of water and smaller glasses of ouzo. You can even go there at ten in the morning, and it was about that time when Homer suggested that Phil do just that. The four architects and I had just had a late breakfast, and Phil was nervously twitching his cigarette and asking Homer whether he should take a flight to Crete for the weekend or hire a car, take in Sounion, and return to Athens for another long night in the Plaka. Homer said, "Just go and sit and have a coffee in Syntagma Square."

Phil told us later that no sooner had he sat down than he saw an old friend of his from Detroit who was going to Delphi with his young wife. They asked

Phil to come along, and they had a warm time together. Phil received a letter from his friends later, while we were still in Greece. They sent this:

Conceived at Delphi

They stole away to Delphi. The couple stayed
where rocks reach out to touch the air
and gods would play if gods did anywhere.
Their bed on the lip of infinity was laid,
and drunk with sky, they clove to mortal frame.
In such a fold a civilization could fare
forth; in such a fold our earthly pair
conceived a child above the olive plain.
Lie peaceful, little baby, in mother's fold.
Much later, when down lies dark upon your face
and stones are dreamt like those, may you be told—
should you be led this reliquary to trace—
they stole away to Delphi. What vapours rolled,
what tale of destiny in this moment of embrace?

ೞ

It was late one evening in the Plaka. The four had found a tavern—a restaurant—toward the end of the Plaka in the direction of the Agora and the modern flea market. In the restaurant were only one Greek family and a few old men. The family, which was poor, to judge by outward appearances, was celebrating a betrothal. Young and old danced, and plates were smashed on the floor. (Perhaps at home they would have such a set for a lifetime.) The three *bouzouki* players might have looked tired by some standards—at least, they had not achieved their dream to be famous—but there was a glow about their eyes when they saw the four. It was like the thousand-fingered dance that they had mastered in order to accompany an evening during which warm breezes and the sparkle around old men's dancing feet met to still the moment in which bliss might otherwise have gone unheeded.

That special evening in the taverna under the stars, Aristotle lost his reluctance. He had never believed in rebirth, he said. He said he had thought there were many good things about Eastern religions, but he could never appreciate reincarnation. Then one night he had had a dream.

In the dream, a finger went to a map of Greece, and the voice of the dream said, "You were here." It was east of Thessalonika, between Thessalonika and Istanbul, just above the sea on the map. Then he began to see: There was a small house with white interior walls. A soldier of the Roman army was passing on, a Christian. It seemed to be about the fourth century, Aristotle said, and a great light filled the house with a sense of resurrection.

"Oh, everybody thinks he or she was important in some previous life," chimed in Phil, who was starting to reel after several Scotches.

"That may be," Aristotle admitted, "but hear the rest of the dream." The finger went to the other side of the map of Greece, north again, but this time just south of Albania. Again, the voice said, "You were here," pointing to a taverna like the plain ones near the square in Nafplion.

Aristotle saw a man with an ordinary calling in life having a good time. "This must have been about the nineteenth century," he said.

Esther, the one woman with us, wrote of Aristotle's experience:

> Into this man's dying hour he peered.
> A soldier he'd lived, a leader of the legionnaires of Rome,
> turned Christian. Then in whitened chambers spread
> a bright and resurrecting light about his home.

Esther, full of wisdom like the Goddess Sophia, was an attractive woman in her eighties. She embodied the feminine spirit. She came from Shropshire, England, originally. Her English heritage, alive in North America, was more recent than mine. Although she had no Greek heritage as I did, she, too, loved Greece.

However, Aristotle had been the one who got them all to come to Greece. Referring to Aristotle's dream, Phil said, "and you mean it was to chase *that* rainbow?"

Aristotle said he felt he was risking a lot to pull all that material out in front of his friends. Homer didn't try to defend him but leaned over and placed his broad hand on Aristotle's shoulder.

"You remember Jung's dream?" Esther said. "He dreamed he was on a journey, hiking in a hilly landscape; the sun shone and he saw in all directions. He saw a man, a yogi, meditating in a small chapel."

Phil burst out on his take on all these things. He said, "You mean that life seems to throw up the beautiful dark-eyed woman generation after generation and over the dark course of history and through persecution like that of the Turks here for four centuries? And the woman I saw in the market today is like the one on the vase of the museum at the Agora!" Then he began to chant, "Long live the dark-eyed feminine," as the four hopped and slid down the marble steps leading from the Plaka into the modern town and their hotel.

Esther wrote:

Greece

I give my warmth to you—
I have plenty for my own.
Rest in my simple ease;
eat my ripened tomatoes,
dip bread in salad oil,
climb the olden steps ,
rise to the heights, and
see my mountains beyond.
Find yourself in all my beauty.

ᘒ

The next day Aristotle was on the trail of his own dream again. He found the small church dedicated to St. Demetrios, just in the shadow of the Acropolis on the hill known as the Areopagus. Aristotle shared the note from his journal:

At St. Demetrios' Shrine

I was meditating on what it might mean that, in a past life, there had been a great light throughout the house of this being as he passed on, and enlightenment. I was working, working, working on the idea. Then I became aware of the blood in my hands. I almost went to sleep. A woman came in in white raiment. Then I saw the light increase inside …. "The freshness of the body": this phrase occurred to me. It was tied to the Resurrection and my experience of the energy field of another person a yard or so away.

This all took place, Aristotle said later, just in front of one of those dark, ancient icons, black with age and covered with silver.

ᘒ

A week later in another town near Patras

Aristotle saw Vasillis, a Greek fisherman he had met several days before.

Vasillis was sitting alone in a café on the waterfront, where people stroll at night. He was drinking a beer, and he looked dejected.

Aristotle listened to him and watched him. Aristotle said, "I have met many wonderful people in this town, but you have taught me the most."

For a moment, Vasillis looked as if he believed him. Then he lapsed back into his sorrow and asked, "How can people laugh at me when I cry?" He told Aristotle that, in his heart and in his head, he hurt. He cried, "I can't stand it anymore." He said he had lied when, a few days earlier, he had told Aristotle that he, Vasillis, had a strong heart.

Aristotle told Vasillis that he wanted to tell him a story and asked him for an idea. "What idea?" Vasillis asked.

"Any idea," Aristotle said.

Vasillis reached to touch Aristotle's shoulder, a simple gesture that gave Aristotle the idea he needed. He said, "There is a young boy. He always wants to please others with whom he has grown up, but whatever he does, it never seems quite enough. The boy tries harder and harder because now he has an inner critic who will never rest. Then, when he is over forty, he meets a teacher who lets him strive harder and harder, moving about a room doing "process work", before the teacher stops his striving. He and another process teacher pin him down so he cannot move—can't so much as stretch his toes. At last, when he is without hope, he feels a hand on his shoulder. It is enough. It is enough for him just to be himself."

Aristotle had put the story together from fragments of people's lives he had known. It seemed right. Vasillis' demeanour changed. Aristotle said, "I will pray that the spirit protectors look after you."

Vasillis replied, "You have cleansed my heart."

ෆ

The next day at breakfast, Homer said he had heard a gunshot and women's screams in the night. Then he asked, "Could the gunshot have involved Vasillis?" Homer recalled the last meeting he had had with him.

He had found Vasillis in the restaurant by the quay where he and Vasillis had come after their first meeting. Vasillis was depressed, unstable, and was crying. He talked about how he had been teased by a few of the men in the town who just wouldn't let up on him. Homer asked him to recall all the photos Homer had taken when Vasillis had shown him the town. That afternoon, Homer had pushed the wrong switch on his camera, and all the film had come tumbling out. As the roll spiralled to the floor, Homer took it up in his hands and played with it as if it were a friendly snake. Vasillis laughed throatily at the debacle.

Esther said that she would help Homer search for Vasillis that afternoon. Someone should be able to tell them, in spite of their limited Greek, what had happened to him. They all agreed to meet that night for supper at the taverna by the sea, where all the local fishermen go.

ɔ

If Vasillis had died, Aristotle thought, it would mean that the simple Christian ethic was unworkable. Vasillis had said in one of their early talks, quoting Jesus, if you have two coats, and you meet a man who has none, then give him one. Vasillis had spoken from the heart, and Aristotle had said that it was one of the truest and most touching things that anyone had ever said to him.

Aristotle went back to his hotel and fell asleep in the late morning. That night in the taverna, he told the others that he had dreamed that all the pieces of the visit to Greece had been torn apart and were strewn over the floor. He rose from the dream deeply disturbed, and he decided to work on the dream. He tore a large sheet of paper into eighteen ragged pieces. On these, he wrote what had affected him during his journey to Greece:

breeze	bliss
the Monk	meanings
water	home
contentment	Greek music
helping	joy in meeting
fortune	hope
clean body	rest
pathways, rocky stairs	air
Vasillis	light

He took the tattered fragments of paper and tossed them about the room. Then he bent down, laboriously gathered each piece from the floor, and began the process of fitting the edges together. Only after a very long period of tedious matching was he able to re-create the whole. He sighed.

Phil, who had so far been absent from the evening dinner gathering, suddenly appeared, his arm around a tired-looking Vasillis. Relieved at having found their friend again, they were all talking again, the four architects and Vasillis. Aristotle was writing on his napkin:

You, too, are rocked by waves and sounds,

and the night reaches its fingers
into your soul. Never mind your religion:
the gods are waves, the goddess, night.

If you are blessed to meet a Greek,
a true Greek, then find one
ready to share the comely nature
these gods, goddesses give to us.

It reaches you through his smile,
his enthusiastic sounds and eyes.
Before you know it, you reach a place—
no words, no thoughts, just music in the heart.

ℭ

And before the four architects left Greece, Aristotle wrote:

The capital of the world
is where the heart is lovely.
Flowers bloom there beside
narrow, rocky stairs—
begonias red, hyacinths climbing.

No one wakes to thoughts
that disturbed the yesterday.
Birds chatter instead
to greet the morning
with its proper hymn.

Why does he smile at me?
Why, she, time to talk?
The gods have given
everything here.
I hear it in my humming.

CHAPTER TWO

Poetry as Markers of the Greek Journey

Now I shift from narrative to poetry to have another take on the events of the first chapter. You may recall the line, when Aristotle was in the Athens hotel and could not sleep that sleep and a dream followed, a dream in which appeared "a powerful spiritual figure from Greece itself, a man in gold robes, a monk." This was Saint Demetrios.

A Saint in My Legs

There is a new spirit—
I felt it in my legs—the dream's old
Greek saint with golden robes, Demetrios,*
He was just so,
the relaxed contemplation
of nothing except
the divine present.
I never knew you would come
like this, Father, joy,
Protector, making thyself
known in an Athens hotel
in the early hours of the morning,
when the crow hissed at meaning,
and I was bereft of familiar
      ambiance.
Just now, for you, Spirit, to come again,

in my legs,
wand'ring the world,
now to be at home
in Thee, saintly Progenitor,
as I begin to be.

* The patron saint of Thessaloniki.

The Areopagus, Athens, and St. Demetrios

One of my favourite places in Athens is a small church on the Areopagus on a hill just across from the Acropolis. It is dedicated to St. Demetrios, a favourite of the Athenians, and he is said to be a protector of all of Greece.

The first time I visited the church, whose interior is not much bigger than a living room, I was struck by the soft light inside at the time of the dying day. It was the beauty of a quiet peacefulness, a composure so deep that it could not be questioned. In its simplicity of form, reminiscent outwardly of a small Japanese house with a porch, nothing was to be added; it seemed always to have been there. Maybe it had, since the early days of this aeon.

When Esther Harding visited Greece for the first time, she was in her eighties. On her way back home to New York City, she flew to England and stayed in London. Bill Kennedy, with whom she had gone to Greece, says that they usually met for drinks before dinner—I would guess in the room prepared for that in the hotel. Bill recounted that Esther had said something completely uncharacteristic for her: "Let's talk irresponsibly."

It must have meant, "Oh, let's let our deepest feelings speak." To tell you the Greeks' story of St. Demetrios is a little like that for me. I can't be literal about it, nor can I let go of it. The saint of Greece, the essence of its spirituality, the mark of its inner sense of its truth and body and form—this is the saint who protects Greece.

It was on the Areopagus that St. Paul, of Christian tradition and Jewish heritage, looked around and said, "I perceive you [Athenians] are a very spiritual people."

M. Esther Harding and William H. Kennedy were two of my mentors. Harding was among the first few Jungian analysts in North America and one of the women writers on feminine psychology; Kennedy grew up in C.G. Jung's home as Jung's ward.

At Demetrios' Shrine

Recalling the light
that spread through all the house
of the dying soldier
in Roman conscript
turned Christian,
a past life of my soul,
as so the dream had pointed—
meditating at this sacred spot
in Athens, dedicated
to a Greek patron saint,
one martyred at Thessaloniki—
sitting before the icon
I almost fall to sleep.
In white raiment she comes,
my half-opened eyes
see the light increase!
She only passes near,
"the freshness of the body,"
resurrection!

Spirits Who Protect

Come abide with me,
Spirits who protect my life and work.
Be my daily presence
as I walk upon the earth.

I have provided a place
on the smoothed "inner ledge"
for you, my Guardian Angels,
That you may alight on this edge.

It overlooks my daily life.
A message I write in the sand
above your shelf contained by cliffs.
Behold, you keep all things in hand.

Previous Incarnations

A dream that one night did come
with finger pointing to earth in Greece
and saying there you once were born
a soldier, and lived, a leader
in the legions of Rome.
There you also were Christian.

And, lo, I looked more closely,
and in his house, three centuries
after Christ, I knew this incarnation
of his was ending, for in all
the whitened, inner rooms
a peaceful light was spreading.

Not only soldier, but waiter,
my earlier lives did take.
A happy man this later one was,
serving people wine and bread.
The finger had pointed as well
eighteen centuries later, bringer of joy.

I travelled to Greece to find these dreams,
knowing my life upon these men made.
I travelled many places, sought out
many souls, and on my path stayed.

The path led to simple folk— fishermen,
musicians, waiters, household mothers.
Each bore some answer great to me.
No need I had to seek out others.

Then crossed my path a statuesque priest.
To him I told the dreams that night, one hand
with finger pointing to northern Greece
and saying it was my earlier life and land.

Into this man's dying hour I had peered,
a soldier and leader in legions of Rome

turned Christian. Then in whitened chambers
    spread
a bright and resurrecting light through his
    home.

CHAPTER THREE

Another Journey Shared with My Family and with Greek Families

The art of living, some have said, is the greatest art. The Greeks have had many years of practice.

We had a month in Greece, mostly in a small town. During that time, I developed a speaking relationship with fifty to one hundred people. I saw them repeatedly over this period, exchanged greetings, and had short conversations on several occasions with many. These experiences warmed me a great deal, and I hope these people also got much out of our relationship.

Nafplion is one of the most scenic of Greek cities. The houses on its narrow streets sport small, iron-grille balconies with brilliantly coloured flowers hanging from flower boxes. There is also a stunning Venetian effect in the boat-shaped stone fortress, the Bourtzi, in the harbour. Nafplion was the first capital of the independent Greece of the mid-nineteenth century.

Shortly after we moved to Nafplion, the tourist bureau sent us to the family of Madame Kotsiopolous. The four of us slept in one room the first night.

Later, in the first ten days, we were invited to the home of an older woman. Our children had bought some pencils in a small shop where she was a clerk. She loved my little daughter, eleven years old, and would touch her and stroke her hair.

The afternoon arrived when we were to go to Mrs Spanos' home. She said to come at about 4:00 p.m., and we woke up two other Mrs Spanoses before we found the right one in Pronia, a subsection outside the old town of Nafplion. We sat and talked with her an hour or so, and she told us about her husband, who had died some eight months earlier. Like many Greek widows, she wore a black dress. I couldn't help wondering to my wife afterwards how the woman's eyes danced, how much love there was in them.

Just before we left Nafplion the first time, I met a man who owned a shop and who had been to China. I took my wife in to meet him because of her interest in tai chi, the Chinese dance.

When he was in his late teens, he had gone all over the world, as Greek men like him do, working on a ship. He had spent time in China, North America, Indo-China, India, and many other places. Now in his late twenties, he spoke of wanting to go sailing again. He had a wife and two children to whom he was devoted, but his heart longed for the roving life.

He could talk about these things—how much he wanted again to go off alone, sleeping cheaply, meeting people. But now he left Nafplion a couple of months of the year and travelled around Greece.

I said to him, "You are Odysseus."

He said, "Yes, we Greeks have it in us."

Archetypes are transpersonal patterns and powers. We meet them in our dreams in the symbols—very powerful symbols—of prophetic leaders, saints, and politicians, to name a few examples. They come in and out of our lives among a cast of many heroes. With this friend, I had the feeling that one of the great archetypes of the Greek people had represented itself so strongly in his soul as to return again and again and impel him to endless journeys and adventures.

Just as we were leaving Nafplion the first time, this man said, "Come and stay at my house." My wife was eager to visit more places, so we went on to other parts of Greece, but we were soon to return to Nafplion.

I was very fond of the man who ran a small coffee shop in Nafplion, Kafe-Hellenikos, where all the men of the town had their morning or afternoon coffee. He was a shy Greek man, grey-haired and slim, an older man, and he smiled warmly. I liked him for his quiet ways among so many extroverted Greeks.

On our return visit to Nafplion, we met Adonis. It was five o'clock in the evening, and he appeared to serve us, dripping from a shower he had just taken at the back of his shop. We ate at his small restaurant three nights in a row because my son, who really liked the cooking there, wanted us to return. Adonis said, "You come to my house, Karathona."

The day came, we arrived, and we sat eating and drinking the retsina he had made. The ocean and mountains were beautiful and idyllic, and people who were able to joke and laugh with the most limited number of Greek and English words did just that. I thought, this is the best: these people and this beauty. I was able to say it. I gave Adonis my sunglasses.

I hadn't known that his invitation was for lunch, and I had eaten lunch beforehand, but naturally, when I was asked to come up from swimming and have lunch with his family, I had that, too.

The retsina he served felt like it wouldn't allow me to rise from my seat. I drank that, too.

What do the Greeks have to teach us? Perhaps it is that some of us northern Europeans and North Americans have not learned to be so tuned in to the joys that these Greeks taught me, that in every transaction with every person is an opportunity for something very human to take place.

Adjustment in this sense is very hard to put into words. It is an attitude; it is what one does when one is abroad and knows the communication is going to be very limited, at least in terms of language.

The Greek people are the masters of this quality. They teach what it means to give. They give and give. Even their music patterns this quality.

I was down at the beach. I tossed the Frisbee to my son, and then I threw it to another fellow there. He was a student from Athens.

We got to talking, and he was interested that I taught in a university. He said I was not as egotistic as many of the teachers he had. I liked him a lot, and I invited him to have supper with us. He couldn't come that evening, but he could the next.

We took him to our favourite restaurant. He enjoyed himself with the children, but he remained remote with me. Perhaps he was judging me along class lines. He told us about being interrogated during the student riots in Athens during the "the Colonels". He spent one week with them and four weeks in the hospital.

Like many times before, I realized this was someone with very high connections in the government. His questions to me regarded whether he had been permanently damaged from his experiences of torture as a captive of the military police.

On the last night, I went to chat a bit with the landlady of the place where I was staying, Mrs Kotsiopolous. She was a woman in her sixties of whom

I was very fond. Her daughter, a woman in her middle years who was there visiting from America, told me that Mrs Kotsiopolous was very unhappy.

It was then that I learned that the other daughter Mrs Kotsiopolous had said was dead was really in a monastery. The old woman was beside herself; she wanted nothing more than that her daughter settle down and have children. As the visiting daughter said, this is, in the eyes of a woman of the older generation, the one thing a woman should do.

It was a complex tale.

The "lost" daughter had a university education, but at the age of thirty, she suddenly removed herself from home and entered the monastic life, where her future contacts with her parents and family were restricted. In fact, even a visit with her parents had to be supervised by the head of the monastery.

The old woman couldn't accept that her daughter had entered a monastery. She had raised the girl strictly, restricting the hours she could be away from home and urging her to go to church.

This was one of the hardest aspects of the situation. Perhaps she felt herself responsible for the choice her daughter had made.

The woman dealt with her feelings by constantly doing very heavy work on the house. She wouldn't even take walks with her husband, who seemed like a very nice fellow, and she refused to see a psychologist. It was something neither he nor the daughter from America could understand, but it seemed the daughter felt her sister had the right to lead her own life.

Shortly after meeting Mrs Kotsiopolous' daughter, I met an American couple outside a movie theatre. They were going to see a late show of *Donald Duck in the West*. I told them not to go but to come with me to the *boîte*, roughly translated as nightclub or bouzoukia.

I hadn't been too interested in this couple when I first met them: I was simply more fascinated if someone was not North American. Still, we got to talking. They loved the bouzoukia, and the man said something of deep relevance to me.

What happens when one travels to Greece is that the unconscious is set alive. One leaves behind some of the time-regulated consciousness of north European and North American life, which allows the unconscious to see the possibilities of the moment and the others who come by.

The Greeks are very aware of this. They watch the hurry and the harassed quality of tourists with amusement, some considerable forbearance, and an understanding that we, the tourists and visitors, cannot really change their awareness.

You see, if you give the unconscious time, it makes things happen.

Marie-Louise von Franz, the Jungian writer, says that the unconscious has a seat of judgment of its own, not unlike the conscious mind in this respect.

It wants things that logical consciousness does not want and would not choose. Its ways are not our ways. For example, if I had set out to have a deep conversation with the American couple, it would never have happened.

Over and over, I had to say to myself: you must not say "no" to life as in Mrs Kotsiopolous' invitation and the impulse to invite the student for lunch. With Adonis at the restaurant, I was a little less sure, as I had had a slight warning or possibly an anxiety dream.

In Greece, I was constantly aware of the unconscious. I was able to live in it. I experience the unconscious, or the psyche, as a medium, expressing a quality of life.

Does travel activate the unconscious?

This brings in "relationship." In these circumstances, one can easily see many qualities in other people that may also be in oneself. Because lack of certainty about language robs one of certainty about the meaning of conversational exchanges with others, two things happen: one has to guess a little, and one has to read the signs of body language, physical expression, tone of voice, and so on.

In the first instance, where one has to guess a little, there is always the danger of projection. I will see the other person as untrusting or trusting, depending on my own state. Since the unconscious is activated and since projection can easily take place, many fascinating events can take place.

For example, my friend Gorgo says that part of what happens on a trip is supplied by actual events and the rest is made up of what the inner person sees with his or her mind's eye, imagination, poetry, wish, and dream.

Because the unconscious is activated during cross-cultural experiences, those experiences become a time of potential growth. Possibilities come, and one can take them or leave them, but one is invariably confronted with the new and different where one may find new meaning.

In Greece, I felt new potentialities of the human being on every side.

Of course, when confronted with the new, people may either go forward into the strange and new or react by seeking the familiar, which may not even exist in their new surroundings.

The most common example of this phenomenon of which I am aware of is visitors in Greece from other countries looking for their own national cuisine—the search for the familiar.

For some, the push the new gives to development and expansion of the personality may be too much. The new culture contains what they do not like, and they remember their home country with relish: it seems the best place in the world; if only we could get back there, things would be fine.

The unconscious is not always kind; it can do strange things to people. It activates patterns that may have been repressed in the home culture, and some of these patterns, when lived too literally abroad, can have destructive consequences.

One time I decided to ask directions in a small hotel. I had lived in Nafplion for several weeks, but one of the churches mentioned in the printed guide eluded me. It was in Pronia.

I got more than I bargained for. The man at the desk said a man would take me there, and although I didn't want to be taken there, I agreed. As I walked along the streets with the man, I learned that he had lived in Detroit. Perhaps, I thought, he had driven a taxi or worked on the docks.

When we entered the church, my guide was enthralled. He spoke ecstatically, pointing out Mathew, Luke the physician, Mark, and John. He pointed to each one, specially designated, more real and particular than the "portraits" painted into the ceiling seemed. They were familiar characters to him, as well known as great uncles, and his expression was full of excitement, mystery, awe.

Another icon revealed Jesus leading Lazarus from the grave in the presence of the sisters who loved him so much. In all my exposure to the stories of Christianity, they had never been more real to me than at that moment.

Each time we went somewhere in the town, a different person introduced us to the shrine or ruin there.

One day we set off for Haghia Moni. We walked over several hills before meeting up with a dusty country road. Finally, we saw a taxi and, when we asked the driver how much further it was, we decided to go the rest of the way by taxi.

We arrived in a very ancient place, where it took some time to rouse someone to let us into the main church. It was all very cloistered. A few nuns stood about, and very old trees grew among stone walks and stuccoed buildings.

One of the nuns met us, just another couple of tourists in her eyes.

When we went inside the church, she said something about Gregory. I said Gregory of Nyssa was my favourite of all the Church fathers. She may have been surprised to hear a person from abroad talking of the Cappadocian fathers.

In front of the icons of this holy place, we found the gold bracelets and rings of scores and scores of people. You might say this is what made the church so valuable. No, this jewellery didn't make it valuable: the jewelry was there because so many people felt the shrine was valuable.

The icons were remote and of persons ancient, yet they were particularly beings of feeling.

The monastery itself was situated on one of the most ancient places in Greece, near a spring where Hera, wife of Zeus, had gone to purify and renew herself in the spring bubbling from the earth after being with Zeus. Hera, you will remember, was Mother Earth herself, the mother of all things.

It wasn't surprising that, when the Christians came, they connected this place, with all its significance, to life and, reaching back all the way to antiquity, to Mary. There, Mary was the mother of Spirit.

We saw these ancient waters as they came pouring out of the hillside. A balustrade supported a trough of ancient rock carved with symbols in sparkling stone. Just where the water poured into the hewn stone bath, a fresh leaf was carried along. Someone always made sure a fresh leaf was there.

We bought a small icon in the rooms where the nuns sold lace and embroidery.

Later on, we walked in the fields far below and saw great pipes carrying water to make the lovely groves of olive trees arable.

One may go to Greece looking for "origins," in itself a religious thing. Religion means linking backwards. It means picking up the links that lie with our past, between ancient things and what is happening to us now.

Why is it that sometimes we feel that we must go to the origins of things to understand them? Looking for those origins took me again to Epidauros in later years.

Later, after we had visited a small chapel in Nafplion, Amy, my eleven-year-old daughter, said, "You know, the gods are alive here." Nothing we, her parents, had said to her before was along this line. It was true. In some kind of way, Epidauros had shown us that.

The Greek Church is full of miracles, although I know this is a subject about which some people have taken a dim view.

I have to tell you a story though. Near the Acropolis, on an adjoining hill called Mars Hill, there is a church that dates from early medieval times. When I saw the building, even before I realized its function, I thought it was one of the most beautiful buildings I had ever seen. Very small stones in shapes of many sizes, often smaller than bricks, were placed in patterns of conjoining rectangles, the unification of which pleased the eye.

The inside was every bit as mysteriously beautiful, although I would be at pains to explain why. Two of my children, Amy and her brother Andrew, age thirteen, were struck in some deep way at the wonder of the place. They were completely captivated by the place and went about placing candles in the various stands before the icons.

An inscription read: On a Sunday morning, when Christians were worshipping inside, the Turkish governor was preparing to shoot a cannon against this building. A thunderbolt hit the powder magazine stored in the Parthenon, nullifying the plan. The praying Christians felt it was St. Demetrios who had come to their aid.

The Greek music I can describe only as uninhibited. The members of the church I attended sang many parts of the liturgy—just ordinary people singing full-voiced, much as tradesmen would do while working at a lathe. All of themselves went into it—there was no self-consciousness—and the tones were as rich and real as those of a father laughing with a child on his knee.

At the end of this month in Greece, Andy said, "It was the best vacation I have ever had!"

Karathona

Adonis's "house" is there
at one in the afternoon
he is already swimming
gold teeth shining
a man who has gone back
to his swimming ancestors
playing the dolphin

then again if you're there at two
Adonis will be offering the pagan
thanks over the food
that comes from the cactus bloom
the olive's harvest and the baker's oven
and retsina to make
all mellow and happy

Adonis's table is a happy place
stretched outside his tent
his wife serves the moussaka

you want to dance
you talk instead
and the words flicker like
the sun on the waves

Adonis's table is a special place
there is great Greek *happiness* here
I look up and see the mountains
encapsulating nature's greatest beauty
Eftehea
I have arrived.

A summer shelter on the Karathona beach,
the Peloponnesos, Greece, 1978

Greece, the Ancient Potion

These old bones of mine,
They don't creak and they don't rhyme,
But they are getting better every day.
These bones are getting better every day.

These old lips have learned to smile,
Just to smile and relax a while.
They are getting sweeter every day.
These lips are getting sweeter every day.

This old heart, I feel it there,
Full of care, it's full of care.
The heart is getting feeling every day.
This heart is more feeling every day.

This mouth of mine, it used to scold
And act so cold, so cold.
The tightened mouth, it's growing mellow.
This mouth is growing ever more mellow.

CHAPTER FOUR

Returning to Greece:
Later Journeys

Dungeon of Athens
The Bus Station

Like a dungeon at four in the morning,
like a wasteland, this section of Athens,
with disabled vehicles, is rusty
and has no hope for a resurrection.

Were I to cry any supplication
at this graveyard of dusty machines,
not a person would be there to listen,
save this plaintiff and an assailant, it seems.
A statement to sound but no audition,
a note one might ring but no hearing.
This station on the outskirts of the city
was closed, said the city bus driver,
mine to wait for a six a.m. departure
alone with a few other creatures,
the unsheltered clutching those walls
unlikely to help if needed.
At the city bus stop another had departed.
This man called after me,
this stranger was there for the talking,
and together we stayed untold darkness.

I have arrived in Nafplion. I am not writing a dream. This time it is reality. I sat on the balcony of my hotel. I could dream of the dreams I have had of here, Nafplion.

Ecclesia Catholic
*A la memoire des Philhellénes morts pour l'Independence**

I went to my famous church,
where my spirit had been reborn.
I stood on the porch and surveyed
the tile roofs below of my beloved Nafplion.
This was the hill I came to
with a mentor in my dreams
and knew it was a sacred place.
Now in walking life on the same crest,
I began to pray,
now my mind unhappy in fear
of war in nearby Crete,
my usual self-protecting
exercises of mind going on between prayers.
I couldn't remember doing anything,
just my body relaxing
an unearthly relaxation,
a pulse near a sleep
of total ease.
Was this prayer?
I knew I was in a place
many had prayed—
Otto of Greece,
and there the tribute to Byron
and all the Philohellenes
who died in the war
to set Greece free.
Was the Greek Orthodox Church
not also the same body
as for my grandfather's baptism?
I relaxed.
I had been waiting a century.

* Inscription at the church in Nafplion to these Grecophiles

I realized later, as I wrote this dream, that the phrase "waiting a century," which had just come into my imagination unexpectedly, was meaningful. At the church, after prayers, I read that King Otto had, in fact, come to that church in 1839 (and brought its tribute to other Europeans), and that was one hundred years before my birth!

There was another connection to the church. My dream of that morning had also been about houses I had recently visited in France. When I visited the church about an hour after the dream, it struck me that there was the tribute to the Philohellenes, mostly French, who had died in Greece during the War of Independence.

Perhaps an ancient city in a modern person's dreams relates to that person's inner life. Nafplion is for me a powerful symbol of a change of life, based upon experience of a spiritual home, that allowed me to experience part of my own ancestral and mystical tradition.

Epidauros, also on the Peloponnesos, demonstrates two important functions that the Greeks added to the city: a place of healing and the theatre. A third contribution to the city is found in Olympia, where the Greeks found a way to give a unity to separate states and even to let war subside during the pan-Hellenic games. Lewis Mumford wrote about these functions.

We first turn our attention to Epidauros. Provision is made for the pilgrim in the hostelry, a way for pilgrims to be received and to stay while they work with the priests of Asclepios, visit his temple, and take part in the cure. Next are the baths in which one is purified, refreshed, and connected to the deeper realities through water, the source of life, healing and transformation.

There are temples and altars of many other deities. If we change our direction now and arrive from the north, we meet the temple of Aphrodite, who is often coupled with Asclepios in the healing shrines. The Yale authority on archaeology and architecture, Vincent Scully, points out that no cure is complete without the goddess of love. One intuitively knows this from psychological experience; when one is touched by love, the greatest internal resources are released. Then one meets the altar of Hermes, whose elongated stone statue is a rectangle with a head at the top and an appropriate representation of the phallus. A herm is often found at mountain passes, sometimes as a pile of rocks that symbolizes Hermes presiding over the gate, the transition, the transformation. One essence of Hermes as phallus is that he comes and goes. The Romans and the people of the Middle Ages called him Mercurius—changeable. As Mercurius, he symbolized a particular relationship to time and events, something like being in the process of the Tao.

When one is ready to approach the temple of Asclepios himself, one makes an offering. Most Buddhist meditations end with a dedication to some higher purpose. As one stands before the temple of the God of healing, one knows healing is possible in some important respect. Healing is not equated with cure but that one will be made more whole, more of one's total self. That will be a change, a step in the process of evolving, the enacting of one's personal myth.

One will see the god Asclepios in his temple, accompanied by a snake. The snake is a symbol of transformation, as in its course of life it sheds its skin and acquires a new skin, but it has many, many meanings. As a feature of inner life, it is full a creature with tremendous power and a mind of its own, so the snake is one form in which the god Asclepios may visit his devotees and pilgrims. The snake also connects the work of Asclepios with that of the goddess whose caves and whose sacred snakes, visiting the sick, brought recovery. Thus, in this most important of the shrines of the Greek god of healing, the forces of the masculine and the feminine both come into play. In fact, one of the unmistakable healing factors of Epidauros is the landscape, the earth, Mother Earth.

Everything about this site leads the eye of the pilgrim back and forth between the wonders of nature and the creative genius of the builders.

When we prepare for sleep—for it is here that the god of healing may visit the sick or distressed person, offering a healing touch or a remedy to be employed—we roll out our blankets on the abaton, the long porch adjacent to Asclepios' temple, and hope for a healing dream.

Just one more thing needs to be said about this beautiful spot. The theatre at Epidauros is itself a wonder. Fourteen thousand persons could be seated, and the crumpling of a paper on stage could be heard in the most distant row. The hills beyond are complemented by the curves of the architectural structure.

Drama complements other ritual healing practices. The drama of Ancient Greece works on the emotions, perhaps stirring a memory of a time when one was fragmented or unhappy, teaching the ego that it is not the centre of the true life of the self. This connection between drama and the emotions may open one to a blessing that comes from beyond the narrow limits of personal wishes.

As great as the Greek myths are, they are meaningful primarily when they connect with modern life. In one of my pilgrimages to Greece, I had the company of my son, and his friend, both then twenty-five years old. I met my son as a man, and he met me as a man. There was a healing in the journey together and in the time spent, which was reminiscent of the ancient gods, Asclepios and Hermes, and the Great Mother.

Asclepios

Of shadows a figure formed
grey, enfolded, robed,
in my afternoon meditation,
near sleep: Asclepios.
Earlier that morning
in the ancient sanctuary,
enclosed by gentle mounds,
with Peloponnesian heat
softened by the healing winds,
I, the pilgrim, had uttered my prayer.

Asclepios appeared in a dream I had the night after visiting Epidauros. In the dream, I was healed of prostate cancer. More than two decades afterwards, in the summer of 2006, I was given radiation treatment for prostate cancer, and it is currently in remission.

Remembering Lewis Mumford's great work on the city, let us now consider the labours of the ancient city. In a village, all the tasks of life may have been done by one man, one woman, their family, and sometimes groups of families. In the city, by contrast, these myriad functions were each performed by specialists. In that sense, the city is a conglomeration of specialists. Everything exists in the city, so those who are best at specializing may be most adapted for work there.

What is virtually lost today is the person who can do all the things for herself or himself. Zorba the Greek is, to some extent, such a person. He says to the bookish intellectual, "Boss, I can work with my hands"; he plays the the santouri, a musical instrument; he mines for ore, negotiates with priests, settles disputes; he represents the whole man, especially when combined with the intellectual Englishman.

In part, ancient Greek philosophy entered strongly into the foundations of Christian theology through the Cappadocian Fathers, such as Gregory of Nyssa, and through Origen.

For me, ancient Greek culture is like the backbone, philogenetically, of western culture.

From Werner Jaeger's *Paideia*, quoting Heraclitus: "Travel over every road, you cannot discover the frontiers of the soul—it has so deep a logos."

England
("The English Part")

Poems as Markers
Poetry and Narrative Together

CHAPTER FIVE

A North American Living in England

Sheltered Island Lands

Ebullient clouds were strewn in rising tiers,
the inwards stairs that reached the unspied dome
and gave a height unknown in other spheres,
expanse to sheltered island lands, to home.
The pastures past the pond went on and on,
the hedgerows lacing greenfield after green,
and timeless ticking cows' tails upon
the garden's bounds affixed a boundless scene.
As upward stairs had swayed my pen to rise,
and nether lands had granted cool repose,
so I was Eye on all of earth and skies.
Can ruddy breaths and sounds these lengths disclose?
    Ah, children's cries, the sweetest music still,
    caught it all, this England, and the quill.

"The Rookery", New Buckenham,
England, 1972

Birds and Fishes

I set a ring of parched stones.
I gathered wood the shade of bones.
I hied me high o'er dimming tide
to lay this fire in eventide.
A day before this thought had burned,
and setting store in dreams, I yearned
to gather driftwood, kindle flame,
this dark and steaming seaside claim.

A lamp awaits the midnight sun
and shelter gives as shelter won.
The nips of light around the base
return my sight to quiet pace.
Then larger twigs begin to boil.
From lamp-lit damp uncoil
the worms of passing summer's night.
Quietly I await the night

to nestle this unsettled land;
from birds to fishes it passes hand,
where unworldly depths and sky meet
each day, plant, and each retreat.
I haven't laughed like this again
or sung sweet heaven's songs, a din
to my very self. This eve I lay
on flats, the chilly lake at bay.

I'll give them back, as all before
have wrested a moment, can wrest no more.
In a glance, I recognize the call
to burn again the flotsam and all,
as once upon another shore,
the day my lyre was born and more,
this speckled star of mine began
and I to loving as I can.

The North Sea near Blakeney

The Rookery

A Norfolk village,
English in every respect,
with its own castle
Saxon,
self-described
as never having been touched
by "Satanic mills"
and all the rest.

Picture a house
on its own lot
with a gate and drive
at the village edge.

There, untrammelled by time,
I aspired to poetry.
The garden was perfect,
the pond
enticing for children.

We had so much there,
but I had my solitude.
Come an afternoon,
I would sit outside
in range of the children's voices,
and labour
to produce a few poems.
This is why
I thought I'd come to England.

A poem maybe,
but the ambiance
is still with me:
the thought to create.

The Village Shrouds

The village shrouds away from clouded moon,
and fog runs the channel of King Street,
hiding present moment, carrying feet
to centuries past, moans of cows, and soon
we wonder where we are. Could be Tirol
or any darkened past, far past the time
of speeding cars and instant talk and clime
of light at night, people in bright foil.
In the rector's house a Christmas tree gleams;
he has to have a tree, a tree for all.
The eight o'clock bell sounds fall
against a thousand tiny beads. It seems
    this fog has brought all years in soft relief
    and with usual memory played the sieve.

A Norfolk Night

The earth receives us;
it is a Norfolk night.
The corner of the old bed
is both vantage and delight
as we two stare and absorb
the wondrous making of the night.

Old trees lining the fields
quiver in the wind's night
and make their stand again,
if ever moved their plight,
connected we know to the still
and living earth this night.

Clouds are driven o'er the sky
and shape o'erhead the sight
of frizzy tendrils, a stream
becoming to space in light,
supplied by our mother moon,
our tend'rest sponsor and light.

The stars, too, appear
in gaps of clouds' flight.
Our mother colours this space
deep blue of night,
lost in stars' messages
to lovers, children bright.

The earth receives us;
it is a Norfolk night.
The corner of the old bed,
both vantage and delight,
as we two stare and absorb
the wondrous making of the night.

The Dark Night of the Year

The dark night of the New Year,
questions that in dust and cramped store
have lain awake waiting, come to the fore,
questions in deep silence one might hear,
before the passing life is pronounced deaf
to all the rumblings shaking mighty souls,
before the body shakes from various tolls.
Nay, before the wind drives one's form as a leaf,
then may one's meaning, like poetic line,
have a clear structure and magical sense
nor fade in breath till the very word
is uttered in grace and truthfulness fine—
for all the solemn years a recompense—
and the presence of the true self actually heard.

How When the Sun Shines in January, It Is Majestic

Silver light breaks through clouds like wings of birds,
Vees of white, swooping downward to earth—
lakeland birds,
green loveliness,
a home.
There are several poems I could write today:
nature children,
how love will leave you alone after you've had it,
how moss turns the rocks green and furry,
how love heals itself,
how the moods change after Christmas,
how life is a fight between love and power,
how in all heaven's moods is a wakefulness,
how when the sun shines in January, it is majestic,
how things change from one day to the next,
    and a hard position taken makes way for compassion
how at the bottom of all big words there
    is just you and me, I and thou,
how the only rotten thing about life is
    that we die just when we are learning to savour
    all its loveliness, past the promise
    beyond the hope,
how one day you wake up and she
    loves you,
how life is a simple container
    transparent, thin, decaying,
and between its folds go on the most
    majestic things ever known to man,
how the strongest impressions happen *to*
    you and there is little you can say about them—
    books don't contain this,
and yet you know it doesn't matter if you don't
    write about it,
because it will never happen again, in the romantic heart,
how even the best of people make mistakes,
how you can wrestle the symbol from
    now to doomsday and yet another

and still another lies behind.
Life has to be simple,
as simple as one's own intuitive grasp of it,
as simple as the courage that says,
    "and now I see it thus; I will act
    from this conviction."

The Rookery, 1973

Thoughts as Clouds

Our human thoughts: how much like clouds near storms
are proud remarks we think to have in stow.
Dark puffs they are, must race for would-be foe
but gathering situation never forms.
Ah, love: the afternoons we fail to count
when nothing striking comes, no sight to hang
the balance on, no vein of gold—just pang
of ser'ate grey; and then the way a fount
can form, pursed of clouds drawing near
purchased of sun itself, in dazzling reign
of light; we sense our streams and skins again
and see the plain become celest'al sphere.
  Oh, winds, what have you with the clouds begun!
  For now our vows as friends have arched the sun.

The Rookery, 1973

All Life a Unity

All life a unity,
said before, I'll say again.
And when by the moaning bar I put forth
and the weed lies reed between my teeth
and axmen lie in wait,
then shall the fortress cease,
the waters part.

And I walked on dry ground.
And the tweedlebird was heard to sing,
loud and ringing,
by the stream.

The Old Stream

The stream of thought had wounded me
"the courage to be." And
I'd thought on it and colloquy
of seminars and far
reaches of reason and
marring of mental sparring—
the agile forgot in bull leaping afar
in Cretan Greece.
Surcease had come in sleep.
I'd woken in afternoon
to find the door to death ajar
and the whiff of the eternal
caught in my nostrils,
a jingle going like this:
    why death at the end
    what was life then?
    never before, never again.

By the Stream

By the stream singing
sweet songs of my youth,
black spirituals bending

the nerves of heaven,
outburstings, cryings,
solemn pleas
uttered in birthing, and birthings be.

In the meadows
I take my leave.
I walk among the daffodils,
am friend to the breeze.
Then I find the road,
small, white stones broken.
The roadmender was here,
entertaining children.
I stand by rushing waters
and hear the roar of forever.
These are my friends.
I shall roll them out on my mat
where the last ocean roll beckons,
and I am heard no more.

I am. I've always been.
Where I was before I do not know.
I have been in the election of the dead.
The sparks of my life were
        struggling centuries ago in
        Greece, and in small prayer
        meetings in England, and later in
        the mountains of West Virginia.
I encompass all my past, dim
        though my awareness be.
My sparks—my best convictions of
        what it is to be me—
        pray, tell, will live on. Those
        who experience them be convinced,
        even as I have been, by others.

I've walked a never-never lane,
supped at a stream of might advent,
slept where paupers craved the rocks to
        cover them from inward wrath.
I've known the stream of consciousness,

wound the way of disbelief,
known every little crook of ruses,
    bent on ensnaring sparks of life.
I thought of his death.
I saw a thrush.
Life has ceased.
The skies opened:
bright light and tender shade,
mossy rock and water trilled
the Scottish mountain glade,
his Eleusinian Field.
The sun gleams
through breaking clouds.
The bells ring
the nine o'clock of
eternity.

Fakenham, Norfolk, 1973
while waiting to move to
Little Melton, Norfolk

King Arthur's Castle

"I suppose that image will fascinate me for a long time. I was struck by how a group of people were tossing rocks under a magnificent, medieval castle—almost in defiance of the rock, its history, its legendary connection with King Arthur, how they were enjoying the simple, elemental joy of youth—something a father teaches his son, and likewise afterwards all forget why, except for the fascination of skipping rocks across the waters."

Tintagel, Cornwall, August 1973

Living Abroad

Twine the rods of Christmas cheer,
twine them far and near.
Twine the songs that bind at hand
loved ones far off this land.

Serve the songs of Christmas feast,
melodies that ne'er have ceased
gladdening winsome hearts as yours,
and spread this warm hearth's lures!

Songs of limitless bounds go on,
connect the far-sought peace
on hills and gentle paths that hold
within me, a Galilee of soul.

She's my hart,* my lamb that's wild
Julie on Mary's lap, Christ-child
in the manger of life's mishaps
formed of Christmas songs and shapes.

Little Melton, Norfolk, 1973

*Psalm 42, RSV

Westwards Fields

Westward fields waving mellow with the touch of wind,
long blades of sun weaving among them,
rustling fondly their new green wheat,
I rest upon you, gentle Uncle.
Would that these rays might reach you
in their bright resurrection from mid-day mist
and past the hour of darkening soon to follow,
touch the stones
of those fellows rising as from their waists
from their sodden graves in the churchyard.
They were about your time!
Some even millers like you,
though your lot had cast its fate
with the inheritors across the sea.
Still, you re-inherit and reap again
as I, a father, think on the father you have been.
The sun on the rim of the earth,
the church on the rim of the field,
the dead in place about her skirts:
Nothing divides me this moment from any of you.

Eyes So Perfectly Human

Mirrored loveliness
awakes the song in the day,
awakes the day in the song.
Beauty in eyes so beautiful
transforms the heart.

Eyes, I have seen thee
in the faces of a thousand friends.
I have loved you
in the eyes of a thousand friends.
You were there in the same
twinkling sheen.
I broke the bread with you, as them.
I loved as I never could have done
had the love of eyes not with you begun.

Norfolk, 1974

Past the Green Pines

Past the green pines, near the ocean,
lies a quiet inner pocket
matted rich with thickest potion,
secret dregs in nature's locket.

Holkham, Norfolk

Setting off from Iona

Past Mull,
hidden in mists,
a ferry churns, and we turn
to face from where we've come:
a link of mountains unbroken reigns,
and beyond a still higher range.
How frail our ship was,
how small the inn;
frailty gains us.
A round stone floor was Columba's bed,
bare timber and skins covering his head.
He pondered these cliffs
and fiercer even Picts
and wondered if the rocks
would fall upon him and hide him from
the Love of God.
But the message knit
in prayer
the message of why he was there,
and slowly the weakness drained into the rock.
He left all in the lap of infinity
to shape within this island fortress beyond
the comely yoke, Christianity.

The Isle of Iona, Scotland,
Spring visit, 1974

The Bird beneath the Stream

Here, where the sun turns the heather grass tan,
here, where nature breeds herself
in the timeliness of conquered thought,
time is a morsel for the gods,
and passion, as the sea's surface
stretches, azure and sunbright,
a mirror image unwavering
toward an infinite meeting with the sky.

I run my fingers through the grass of words
and pull out the prickle of sadness,
delight upon weeds that have their place
where no eye of man has them in its slant.
I have seen a little pink flower
grinning on a stem no bigger
than a fledgling's wing bone
and heard a wren warble
from beneath the thickened mat
where a stream runs singing to the sea.

The West Coast of Scotland,
Spring visit, 1974

Holyrood Castle

sundered, right up against sky light,
might of rock, pinnacled defence
sewn inside this ancient glen,
sure to sight
invading ships on the shore below.

ah, I have seen you on a summer's eve,
the meandering wooden fence
amongst the friendly trees,
the bouqueted ravine
sporting Cinzano ashtrays on canopied tables,
folk lingering with the lilt sounds
of the parade band,
strollers.

when the crowd tensed,
the soldier jumping turrets
searching the hidden
for You Know Who*,
invader of railway stations
foe to the unwary throng
banner missing,
cause effaced in a tyrannical blur.

Edinburgh Festival, 1974

* bombers of the time

Edinburgh, Edinburgh

Evening sun sand, pink on one great
standing stone immortal,
under porticoes fashioned more for Rome,
hiding splendour here
under some wizened breath,
touching some note which won't be heralded,
yet ever more succulent,
as escapable as
the magic of the shaded pediment,
the stately garden
flowers a deep brown rose,
touching tones uncharted.
What am I to do?
I'm looking over my shoulder
and seeing Rome,
the entowered mausoleum
of western remains.

Highland Lilt

Astounding, the peace I feel,
knowing the suffering of the day,
the countless hours rocking with fears,
the ought, the shouldn't, and the may.
I gloss over that now,
for music has held me in its sway,
guided the torn ship of mind
into this quiet bay.
It was bonnie lass, and lilt
and Highland pipes that play
that wooed me to the brightening night
that gently over us lay,
Clear as a bell she sang,
Pure as shepherdess, aye,
singing over the clearest of lochs
as if the world's first day.

Inverness, Scotland, Summer visit, 1974

It Takes Dialogue to Make a Poem

I turn my steps homeward
and homeward I go gladly.
This little journey—ah, well,
you see it has cured me.
I've never been gone for long
the heart didn't yearn for Cyndy.
Being up here in Scotland—
well, it wasn't the same
as when she was wi' me.

Plymouth

Plymouth.
To cross a sea
for religious liberty.
Liberty. Liberty.
The thought went pounding
through my head
and how a new country was
founded on it and other
sacred moments.

Many moments of human sacrifice
and daring go untold.
They are lived, sustained,
contained in men's thoughts.

We all have great moments in our lives,
when we have got up for a son,
warmed the house for others' benefit,
prepared the food.
These are sacrifices worth
the noting.

Plymouth, Devonshire, a visit, 1975

Memory Quintessence

The fourteenth century reliquary,
silent, many-sided, cone-capped
remnants within God knows what,
lavished in the stone of its day
and intended forever.

Surrounded by protective grove
of magical, knotted and ancient
trees,
intricate leaves,
giving home
to flying souls, their weighty weightlessness,
grounded in these.

December dusk has laid you,
medieval city,
where the twilight of years,
the haze of timelessness,
and I—on this, its third day—
can be turned, returned
to some event three December centuries past
in this very churchyard—
allotted a new me now
can I ever guess what?
Across the way my bus is pulling
to its stop.

Norwich, Norfolk, 1975

A Lapis Poem

The sky, medieval blue
(lapis tinted unfading in mind),
timeless clouds,
beaming light faces,
smiling,
teeming promise on our world,
medieval painter certains—
over the infinite landscape—
God's rule!

She, in blue, she medieval
face pure,
I have searched in a thousand faces
for thee, solely pure, pure soul,
Madame Earth,
Mary.

The National Gallery, London, 1976

Quiet Den among the Yew

Quiet den among the yew,
Violet-scattered place
tufted green where
the mower's scythe must be
quiet, and he bend with knee
for fear of razing any stone.
The dead lie here,
but it is not for them I come.
Your majesty hovers here
in the simple green
watchways of the soul,
I fear not here
for any bended knee,
nor trust the loop of salvation
fall outside my sphere.
I am at home here
in this English churchyard.
I cherish no other.

Little Melton, Norfolk, 1976

The Winter of No Relenting

Like a winter of no relenting,
like a song in a flat key,
this wind blew stealthily, entering
the back door, unnerving me.
It was made of hate,
hate where no loathing
reached to an end and stopped
or met the foe imagined to be.
Only in the quiet pose
was it trimmed;
there, where truth knocked,
did I know he was unformed me.

It went deeper, this chilling wind,
deeper to where the promise
of tomorrow bayed,
deeper in the guts of marriage,
where it would seem
neither could live with the other's path,
spiritual, except in that respect,
turned knife edge in the heart and found the dark.

Little Melton, Spring 1977

Upon Taking the House by the Sea

This dim morning,
this bright star,
this star, this inspiration
this moment.

The beeches shattering with light
in a thousand flakes
and shattering again, again,
hung together with
life.
Joyous afternoon for northern creatures.

I.

Fate has seen fit
in this near thirty-fifth
anno bonum
to lift
me from boredom
worn soul-dom
near the fountain
never kissed.
Fate has seen fit
to lift
the tar that glides my eyes.
Fate, my fortune star,
has seen fit to lift my eyes
so far, so far,
far, far—
would you believe it—
to the polestar!

II.

Parkéd on that beach
that reaches
no island breaking
to the crown,
the crown of earthen pull,

need I ask
how I have
come here, come here.
No peasant screams,
no hearts grind,
await streams
of thought pined
and scented burning.
Ah, yes,
it is a tale
how came I here
  running up the path
  to the ocean,
  my panting leaping motion,
  sign reading
  "Warren Woods"
  plaque recalled
  from some dream
  some years before,
  tall greenness
  line, before the door.

III.

(I believed she was here,
that one who restored me to faith in myself;
she visited
—no longer to worship you in this way.)
He kneeled,
posed as rising flower,
cupped the manifest blessings
of this his fateful hour
in his hands,
saw the trickles run
beside margins of loveliness
near valleys of strain,
past the waterfall,
cascading toward the All.

Sheringham, Norfolk, 1977
(house not taken)

Piero della Francesca's "Nativity" and "Moonraker"

Piero della Francesca,
blessed with an authentic nativity
heralded by real people,
and Joseph, raising his crossed foot.
The cow looked with amazement.
I never thought an artist could
have a bird catch in its tilt eye
things unutterable in sublimity:
child adorned by the ardour-crowned
mother, a majesty of devotion.
I laid my head on the rock bench pillow
and knew this picture was
five centuries ahead of its time—
the trapezoid roof shaping
figures of four-folded wholeness,
our magpie perched thereon
waiting the awaited.
Green shoots came from the ground below.
the lowly was never more
powerfully enunciated in the poetry
of a cow's stall.
But Piero, more than all,
gave me ground.

Such ground our age rejects,
caught with the dream of
space beyond earth,
linking stations for satellite docking
planetary creations of Cape Kennedy.
Rejects, our age does, dirt and cows
and babies and plants,
old men's rounded feet,
small birds who recognize holiness.
Has a dream out there
that takes tons of combustible fuel
and synthesized metals
to create a docking.
Why is man's heart in space?
What does he hope to find?
Never a nativity.

*The National Gallery,
London, Summer 1979
before returning to North America*

CHAPTER SIX
Returning Many Times to England: Pilgrimages, Peregrinatio

New and More

Poems of England

England Redoubled

So strong the nerve
that links me to England,
so vital the cord
that binds me to home,
a home I've only
touched upon this lifetime
with gentle journeys
and years numbered in a week,
but the kind of home
England is, is more.
'Tis made of centuries
numbering weeks,
all the harvests of corn
counted in a millennium,
all the crushes of crowds
till Parliaments rebounded,
all the crowns of mercy
and not inclement weather,
all the crosses of saints
and holy scoundrels' speech,
a tone of democracy
and undertow of privilege:
these are my England.
They are in me.

Ah, England is more
'Tis my friend Niel,*
a watchword of sanity,
of a new spirit respectful
of truth of inner life,
not wayward with image
nor acknowledging coyness,
but betting on authentic,
a scholar of the old like me,
bent on unravelling our place
in the now problematic
and future completedness.

This one place is home
for my new spirit.
'Tis my friend Niel's,
where I can speak freely
of what I have done.
I know no courtesy thwarted
by ungenerous glance.
I know no belittling,
whatever the name I give
or accent, view, or class,
I only know I am home
with what I have done.

* Niel Micklem, Jungian Analyst

Cambridge

An afternoon when raindrops dot my page
and we sit about on Cambridge lawns,
needing nothing other than to gauge
the river's level of peace at St. John's,
for the River Cam, though old, is new
and newly makes our minds all free from care.
Ours the watching 'neath the willows' view,
ourselves with watchfulness we find repair.
Solitude is such a blessed state,
yet e'en its very bliss can be improved
when your head on my shoulder rests its weight,
and round the shadows muse is here beloved.
    Fond memories like those a lifetime worth
    When we can be together here on earth.

A Black Box in Cambridge

In Cambridge gardens' peaceful summer sun
a forceful image presses on my mind—
those ancient steps to lapping water run,
and there a tiny trunk of black I find.
Oh, why appear its form as though for me?
I know! 'Tis time to publish what I have,
my attempt within the hidden to see,
and in England's noble language, to vouchsafe.
In St. John's majestic evensong,
the choir spinning sound from Byrd's own pen,
I find that for which I long;
they sing in wonder of Virgin, love of men.
    In the sacred garden's now surprising hue
    'neath the stained Rose, a Gardener in view.

The Couple at Ely

Love turned its form
as a design intricate—
simple, lively Romanesque tapestry in stone
their love was.

He shared the life
that walked so lightly,
impressed in her step,
where no heaviness stalked,
so subtle the spirit in her chest.
He wondered for her,
for the only other like her
was eighty when like that.
Needed she a refuge for this spirit?

In the morning he was to leave
on still another sojourn.
The couple shared their dreams—
hers about him, his
about their meeting up again.
Love turned its form
as a design intricate,
Romanesque, leafy, light in stone-
caressing vines, leaves curling outward,
drinking in sun
in the caring, meeting,
turning stone to life.

Seasonal

The sun is dying;
darkness reigns.
Life could cease
should this chain
of events go on,
yet collective memory
knows better.
Archetype of returning glory
bursts the night,
taming cold,
measuring need,
breaking the hold
of grey, listless
dread of death.
The spark of light
hints at rebirth.

Divine Source
in our very breast,
preserved us.
We know the blest
rebirth in soul,
always awaiting
to break through
in our awakening,

This season, trusted
for love of friends,
what awaits?
Our spirit to mend.

Canterbury—the Darkness

We have our place here
under all this rock,
crowned with all the colours
gleaming through windows,

We have our place here—
belong to this earth raised o'er us,
reminding us of the other
creatures who inhabit the ground,
Our kinship with them
who walk on foundations of stone.

Our place is beneath the earth,
our bodies like those of moles,
reverberating in sound
as earth nestles on us.

Like alchemists are we here,
for stone has been transformed
as space admitting light,
building whole our "stone".
Here Jesu among us—
divine monad in matter.

We're in the incorruptible stone,
in sight of earthly things
become the bread immortal
and singing ecstasy.

Comforting earth here,
how can I stand on earth?
Am I welcome here?
Then a figure appearing
a prophet his form, protector
like Jeremiah said,
"God's presence is here.
It is in your life."

Winchester

Touches of tenderness met by the river's edge
the outstretched arm from the shoulder binding in
love
where ducks waddle and greet and shove
the current 'hind them—gone the need to trudge.
Weary trav'lers look for home abroad;
it comes in unexpected, but here and now
fishermen had their peace just here and stood
where I am ambling now, as Keats did trod.
Such labours landscape puts aside somehow.
Haven't known such encouragement as friend,
my lifetime partner, she did give to me.
These same meadows has transverséd she,
call to beyond, call with no end.
     Tenderness nests in the heart evermore
     and shows the fullness life has in store.

Sheep at a Scottish Retreat

A sheep, a sheep and
other little sheep—
these pass along a land
of vast expanse.
I wonder how before I
missed the chance
to be guided in heart,
tending to keep
to busier roads, amiss
and more dark
ways, ungentle, and
spurious routes galore
in work and play and
always to do more.
"Yours are well-trod
ways," I then remark.
"You're always close
and separate of kind—
we in our world have,
too."
Our ways are not so far
as we construe:
mother, babe, human
and divine, find.
    Oh, Lamb of God, who tak'st away our grief,
    smile on the little, the soul, and thief.

Kagyu Samye Ling Tibetan Centre, Eskdalemuir,
Scotland

The White Knight and the Green Knight *

I carried you down the Slingun,
searched for you on the borders of Kost,
wept by the weary Cyril,
marched with might mercenaries
down edges of Ebb plain,
sacked Goths,
and stabbed viziers
the Caliph had maintained.
Low, I searched where the Brandywine
twined with the Ebb
and flowed toxic past Malibu.
Mighty warriors were my steeds,
and Samalith, allowed as
he had never seen such Love,
driven to find thee, dismounted
in stupor to grasp thy hand.

Contrary nightfall maintains
itself, green his coat
and ever searching
through algae-stained
murky pond moss
difficult to cross.
Replied he:
"Ever the sword-bearer, I
leapt the Hellespont of Love
to serve thy image.

"Where persimmons grow in plenty
and wrathful fields of poppies,
clematis, and white bindweed,
these green and glorious companions
were my preserves as I passed
continents and sea waters on my left
and limped down the lifeline
of hopelessness, filled with despair
at not finding thee."

---

*   I always liked "Kubla Khan"

77

"That apple of Joyfulness
I left unmunched
when the controversy
among the Knight-field
sped into war,
and blackness subsumed
the Camelot of our once mind-
sweet dialogue. That fruit
that savours Truth,
severed from the Vine.

"Now met, thou faithful, White,
like two pillaged nerve channels.
Exhausted, I nearly fall
as I reach for your clutch,
having dreamed of none else
these many and suffering years
since the twain were split.
I, Green Gawain,
Comely in love of friend."

Searching, too, I, White,
down the borders of Dwarfsville,
where sputtering mouths mutter
the conflicting directions,
and no one has seen the green
nor interpreted thy exploits
in the lexicon of gallantry,
I fast faced the North Wind
in the Siberian plain of bleating
friend loss.

Gawain, I've loved thee
since those days in court
we both loved the same woman
and served the mighty Arthur.
Noble our lust for Truth,
consummate in hope to
find the tinned and silver cup
touched by our Lord's own lips.

Never out of mind
this ballasting, bare hope
in the divine and lust-free hope
to serve the King and God and thee,
my friend, whose blood
runs in veins prepared by
solitary nuns in Greece
a thousand years ago,
after our Lord's death.

"I service the high roads
and walk where prickle
may tear the flesh of my dear horse,
limp among the brush,
and brandish the sword
I, Green, dedicated to that Queen
who inspired our hope
in the everlasting crucible-bent cup.

"I sing of thee
when branches bent me in,
and I lumbered among the thicket,
searching the way,
thinking light and the next horizon
might bring me sight of thee
or some signpost
and inspiration of your whereabouts.

"Labour of love and of fasting
serveth the King and our Lord's holy blood,
a day when flaxen-headed infidels
nodded in disbelief.
I so clasped your image,
had walked so far empty on the shores
of that north coast."

Should I put in words? Actions
you require them not.
Should I notice syntax of love avowals?
It is beneath my thought.

I savoured thy noble brow.
I lasted the while of my pilgrimage,
and now I live to embrace Thee
fellow knight, physician, brother.

Norwich, Norfolk

Norwich, in East Anglia, is a medieval city, and it is said that Norfolk was never really touched by the Industrial Revolution.

The old city centre was my familiar place for daytime work for many years. There, as many as sixty beautiful medieval churches were built of the local flint, and they still stand in the small area within the old walls of the city.

Norwich was also the home of Julian of Norwich, a female theologian; of Edith Cavell, the early nurse; and of Elizabeth Fry, the Quaker reformer of mental hospitals and prisons. The family of Elizabeth Fry still regularly attend Quaker meetings in the old meeting house in Norwich. My office at Friends World College was nearby.

Upon returning to North America, I dreamed of a medieval Norwich hospital that was joined to a chapel. In my dream life, I returned to this place in different forms, sculpted by the dream, over a period covering more than two decades.

Accompanying the dream was always a sublime feeling and the realization in the dream that "Oh, I am here again." Trailing off from the bare chapel was an area of dirt that contained prehistoric bones.

A Scene like Norfolk
In a Seventeenth-Century Ruisdael Painting

The vast lands and a single steeple
rise to a more vast sky,
yellow fields, and thin line
of green hedgerows, margin of the known.
Such art in growing grain
and in all else in humans' yearning,
yet the comely landscape's scope,
as far as we can here see,
lies balanced by heaven's heights.
The bounteous, sublime clouds point
to no end of God's territory,
or emptiness generating life.
I placed myself in that scene,
surrounded on all sides and above
and a small road before paving—
no land yet levelled by machine.
It's as we always were,
as we always have been.
The present year with its toil and strain
not so critical as was supposed
in view of something this timeless:
ample context for easing mind.

North America, 2009

CHAPTER SEVEN
Conclusions for the Time Being

Following are some instances of how England and Greece may be experienced when we are not in those physical places. They may become a part of us, of our imaginations; they are imagined in North American contexts, as England is imagined in my numinous, small-group experience and in a dream at a crucial time.

England in my Garden

I found England in my backyard,
the mossy tips round ancient sites,
immense gardens storing visual delights,
sanctified buildings glowing—even the bard!
I found historical pathways to famous places,
nooks and crannies where fav'rite visionaries slept,
castles and stones, time's stories kept,
I walked in England and felt her sacred spaces.
No more do I depend on outer forms;
England, an inner world, is for me,
beyond the bounds of happiness, the limitless weaves,
and marks set by thoughts are passed, and harms
put in place, inner spirit free.
Reverie, more than England, my soul perceives.

North America

Passion Repossessed

In mind, back to Norwich Cathedral:
the cold, dank English night,
furrows of fog about,
epitome of death, yet
vibrant human feelings, too.

Now, another Sunday eve,
so much has passed this day—
psyche's intensest moments.
What to do? My group, adieu,
mine the wine press of thought.

Clever, well I ought to be,
yet the emotions hang about.
I might as well yield
the familiar animals wish in,
others having had *their* flight
(of fantasy) unobstructed by me.
Now my own need to roust
and in this dark interior chapel
find their rest safe in the night,
protected in hay's steamy glow.

Is it I, only I?
Am I closer to others than I thought?
I sit down to tea
with myself.
Eliot, please join in.
You've known the East Anglia churches,
and now I introduce
a wild new brand of group,
and in its trail
of group dialogue: numen.

North America

This poem is one of many postscripts on Greece written in North America. It is from a dream on the eve of the Gulf War. Months before, I had anxiously watched the war's preparation while I was in Greece and the Mediterranean.

Revelations by the Fire

As the log opened,
fire bright candescence flamed
there in the cave-like hearth.
The brightest light,
Dios prepared to announce
its surprises in the world.

The worst news
Dios might still turn 'round.
An intuition like this,
the hottest flame,
brings inside me a child and joy.

World's suffering's
beyond me.
I can't contain;
only one big as world
can—

Dios, eternal in the flame,
in the word,
and in the heart
can.
Kyrie Eleison,

open hearth,
open me
to what is newly
arising in me.

This, the wise man,
old and green,
wearing moss on his sleeve

who met me in a dream,

just before the crossing
where the road
widened past the wood,

and I knew
he had been preparing
some course for me
just by his way.

What lay before me ...
more, more being like his,
more ripening,
his preparing.

I remembered the way
through a second wood
to the quiet garden
with the lily'd pond centre

to the place of learning,
the wise old man's school,
where quiet is contained in knowledge
of the self within.

The mystery is there:
he's waiting in the woods,
fire ready to burn
child to be born.

By the crossing,
before the step, I found
a wood growing,
a long staff

like the walking sticks
by Jung's door,
opening into
the guide's house,

Woodsman, then like Jung,
the step beyond
opening
into the greater way.

Were I to tell you
of the favours Dios gives
his children,
you'd see the fire,
as these other dreams, too,
Dios gave to me:

The Greek priest
about third century
in the portal I passed
glanced barely at me,

but I saw
he had my face,
the thinker
with consummated glance.

Then my vision reached
that rift beyond
o'er which it is said
none passes and returns,

glimpsed beyond of after life,
spellbound faces
celebrating,
bright garmented,

ancients and moderns,
poets, philosophers,
schooled in Athens.
How could I return?

The dream did, to more modern day;
before my group
was to start,
I stopped by the Greek church.

No longer leaning by the door
I took a seat,
then all were filled,
and the holy assembly's
procession began.
Was it Christ's
or Saint Nicholas's,
rescuer from perils, joyful?

Beside him, flaming-
haired woman or man or
Archangel Michael, and
I woke on Christmas morn.

A deeper reality
dreams me.
I have seen his face—
face as of the living priest
of the living Dios, or All.
Does that living reality
yet burn a miracle
for all who yet
stare into its incandescent glow—
world waiting
in us
to heal itself?

And These Reflections in Closing

Zorba is his own man when it comes to his imaginative pursuits. He tells his Englishman employer, in effect, "Boss, you don't possess that part of myself that lives in my playing the santouri."

Especially in the film version of the story, Zorba espouses a life free of family obligations. However, George Zorbas, on whom the partly fictional character is based, did have a wife and children. To his great sorrow, his wife died, but he married again late in life and sired more children.

Perhaps the conflict is expressed even more poignantly in the other character, the bookish Englishman—that is, if we see him as an expression of the narrator in the book and perhaps, behind that, of the writer/artist and even Kazantzakis himself.

Zorba espouses avoiding the sin of not going to a woman when she calls you. Like many men, he never understands that the call of a woman may be a call from his own inner feminine side, which includes his imaginative, creative being. Further, the Englishman stands in contrast to Zorba: he is sensitive in an inner way, a writer who reflects on his experiences with Zorba and turns them into art and imagination, which are soul qualities.

Zorba is outwardly irreverent with the priests in the monastery, yet he gives expression to a wonderful, immediate kind of wisdom. In the face of the outer failure of his plans and schemes, he is able to dance and laugh to celebrate the transcendent joys of friendship with the "Boss."

They make a whole, Zorba and the Englishman: Zorba involved with a tremendous élan, the Englishman steady in his spiritual quest like Kazantzakis in his own life.

Zorba may be the body, the passions, the flesh, yet it is to the Englishman and narrator that we owe the story, the refinement of the story and artful prose—surely expressions of the writer's spirit. In this masterpiece, Kazantzakis is working on the conflict of spirit and flesh, which constituted his life's calling. He creates the pose of opposites in the human soul.

This book, *Spirit and Flesh*, is a reflection on the meaning in our lives, of our attempt to bring together the opposites in our own flesh and being. With all the passion with which we may emulate the "Greek" part, and all the love we may have for the "English" part, we may yet be, in our individual ways, the alchemical processes of mysterious union.

Other Books by David Roomy

Inner Work in the Wounded and Creative: The Dream in the Body.
London: Penguin/Arkana, 1990.

Inner Journey to Sacred Places.
Raleigh, NC: Pentland Press, Inc., 1997.

Muslims like Us: A Bridge to Moderate Muslims.
Lincoln, NE: iUniverse, Inc., 2005.